Volume One

I0481690

The Copywriting Business Formula

by Lukas Resheske

The Copywriting Business Formula:

How To Build A $250,000/year Freelance Copywriting Business From Scratch

Congratulations, you are officially in a client services business! As a copywriter, you are delivering work to a client...and there are only two primary drivers of your entire business. Those two primary drivers are **getting clients** and **delivering work**.

You're paid for the <u>output of your time</u>. If you're doing things with your time that are not actively producing an output, you are *spending* that time, just like you'd spend your money.

<u>You get paid to write copy</u>. The client pays your invoice, and you're obligated to produce the deliverable. **Any** time spent not working on that deliverable is time spent on non-output producing activities...aka: **unpaid** activities.

To fully realize the income potential of being a freelance copywriter, you need to focus on removing yourself from the non-paid activities involved in these Primary Drivers as much as possible. Every minute you spend on tasks that aren't revenue generating is time you're taking away from your life, your hobbies, your family, and your income.

How? Think about it this way: If you want to earn $250,000 per year as a copywriter, you need to make $20,833 a month. If you want to work 10 hours a week, that means you need to make ~$5,200 a week, or $520/hour.

But wait...you need to be PAID to work those 10 hours. So what happens when you spend 8 of those 10 hours doing administrative, legal, accounting, or prospecting activities? What happens when you spend several unplanned hours on the phone with a client that isn't productive?

If you do the math, when you waste 8 hours, you need to make $5,200 in 2 hours. That's $2,600 per hour. Your rates don't magically increase when you waste those 8 hours...so you're going to come up short. That is why you need to systematize and automate as much of your business as possible. Because, when you don't...you're stealing money and time from yourself and your loved ones.

You can build these systems in two specific ways. The first way is to imagine you're going to **sell the business to another copywriter**. That means that you will sell the business to a person who can do the same exact job that you can.

The second way to build the system is to build it as if you could sell it to anybody. That means you'll be able to sell the business to an investor or bigger company, primarily because you've removed yourself entirely from the responsibility of writing copy.

The first way is what we'll be discussing in this book. There are plenty of online courses available to start and grow an agency...but for us freelancers, we often like the autonomy and simplicity that comes from operating solo (or as close to solo as possible)

Now, once you make that decision, we can get into the book.

This book is divided into 2 parts. Part One is about the principles behind a copywriting business. I need to get philosophical on you first...but if you want to skip that and get to the tactics, go to Part Two, where I talk about the "How-To" of each system that you need.

Also, this book was originally spoken in audio form, and then transcribed. For Volume 1, the content will still sound "spoken". In subsequent volumes, the text will be edited and refined to more suit a written book.

First, we'll start by talking about getting clients. We're going to talk about a couple key factors. We're going to talk about positioning. We're going to talk about your ideal market. You're going to talk about offers and leads and pricing. We're going to talk about high-ticket selling and how to do it, and then we're going to get deeper into the tech, the systems and processes and the business model that you're going to be using to be getting these clients. Finally, we're going to finish up with the niche that you choose to be in, and how to do proposals.

Then we'll talk about delivering work, which will focus on the systems you can create that make writing consistently good copy, easier. These are lifesavers for the chronically busy, but also highly important if you want to maximize your ROI from freelancing. The less time you spend figuring out how you're going to write...the more time you have to make money from writing.

In Part Two, I've compiled a list of different systems you'll need to build, and some ideas on how to build them for yourself. You'll need to modify this information to fit your personal needs...but the skeleton is usable by anyone.

Positioning

Positioning is incredibly important for a freelancer and for a client services business in general. There is always going to be a power dynamic between the client and the freelancer or the service provider, and that power dynamic is everything. It is who controls the situation, who is calling the shots, and basically, who's being used by the other person. Now, there are good power dynamics and bad power dynamics, and usually a freelance relationship with a client starts off with a bad version of a power dynamic. This is what I call the status quo, and it's when clients hold all of the power. The status quo and the client's holding all the power is bad for both the client and the freelancer because when a client holds all the power, they're assuming that every decision that they make is correct, according to their marketing or their business. They are negating any expertise that the freelancer is bringing to that part of their business, and they're usually doing things extremely transactionally, extremely narrowly and myopically around the specific project that they want to get done. Versus a new option, where the service providers hold the power.

Now, as service provider, their main goal is to do the best job possible in the shortest amount of time for the most amount of money. The reason they want to do the best job possible is because when you are a service provider, then a lot of what you do relies on your reputation. There is a direct incentive to do a really good job as a service provider, because if you don't do a good job, then your reputation takes a hit. That's what a lot of clients don't necessarily realize or at least jump to the next step and think, "Oh, okay, this is why it's motivating their actions." As freelancers, we know that that's true. We know that it's not just about getting the most money for the least amount of work. It's also about protecting your reputation, and so when service providers have the power in the power dynamic, it allows the situation to flow much more smoothly, and here's why.

The client usually has an idea of what they need to get done, or they have an idea of what the problem is in their business. When they come to you, the freelancer, or a service provider, looking for some sort of service, they usually have some idea of what the solution is that they want. So if they're experiencing a problem in their marketing, they usually want to enact some sort of solution like a lead magnet or an email sequence or something like that. The issue is that when the client sees a potential solution to their problem, that potential solution might not be the best solution in the moment. When you rely on the expertise of a service provider to come in and give you perspective on what the problem is and how the best way to solve it is, then it works out for everybody. The service provider is seen as an expert and an advisor, and the client gets a better result at the end of the day.

It may be that the client pays more for the solution that is really necessary, but when you think about it in the context of what they're trying to do, as in they're trying to solve a problem, they are trying to fix something in their business, then the real value comes from getting that thing fixed, solving the problem, or accomplishing the goal that they originally wanted to do, not in the actual doing of whatever work was presented in the beginning. That's why having a service provider own the power in the power dynamic is valuable for both parties, because obviously the service provider can get paid more for a higher amount of value that they provide, but for the clients, they actually get the result that they're coming to a provider for in the first place.

Now, how clients perceive power and authority. Clients, when they're approaching the freelance relationship, they typically see a person that is going to do a job for an hourly rate, very similar to an employee, only they don't have to pay taxes on this employee, they don't have to do any sort of HR with this employee. It's a very cheap employee for them, so they approach it from a project and hourly rate type standpoint. When they approach, however, a consultant, or an expert, or an advisor, usually that person is someone they're approaching for advice or guidance on it. Something, the price isn't really on the front of their mind. They're concerned with problems and value at that point rather than a project and an hourly rate, so when they approach a freelancer, you do not have a very good power dynamic, but when they approach an expert, an authority, or an advisor, then you do have a power dynamic.

As you can see as we move through this getting clients portion, we're going to be focused on increasing the level of power and authority that you have as a freelancer into that of a consultant, an expert, an advisor for these clients. That's how to gain power and authority ethically and quickly. The mental shift that a client has around you actually happens before you ever interact with them. It's very difficult to change the perception of a person who's already interacted with you, so if you've charged someone $25 an hour to write copy for them, it's going to be very, very difficult for them to see you in the light of a powerful expert or as an advisor. It's just the way human nature works. The fix to that is, you have to come into their state of consciousness as an expert, as an advisor, or as someone who can consult them and help them solve their problem.

The way to do that we'll talk about in a little bit, but it comes from publishing excellent content. It comes from being referred from other people in a certain way. It comes from how you present yourself in general to the client, as in what they perceive from your social media presence, and how you talk on the phone, and everything about your operation. You actively try to show as much power and authority as you can in every step of the relationship, even through the payment and delivery of the work, because, like I said, this power dynamic going back and forth between clients and freelancers, it's always a give and take. If at one point during the process you slip back into employee mode and not into consultant mode, your client will sense it, they'll pounce on it, and they'll start treating you that way, and they will very, very quickly never go back.

Ways to lose power in the relationship. Now, there are very tangible ways to lose power in a client relationship. One of those ways is to defer to the client in matters of your personal expertise. It's when you say, "I don't know. What do you think," when you start losing the power, when you're talking specifically about your expertise. If you're a copywriter, and the client asks you a question about conversion rates for this particular piece of copy, if you say, "I don't know. What do you think," it lowers your power.

If you allow them to increase the scope of a project beyond what was originally agreed to, if you break expectations or deadlines, all of those things radically reduce the power that you have in your client's eyes. It's very difficult to gain power back once you've lost that power. You can set new expectations and meet them, but think about it in a one-to-ten ratio. If you break an expectation for a client, you're going to need to meet 10 different expectations in order to make up for that one break, and that's why it's so absolutely critical to never break an expectation and be able to control all of the expectations.

Now, the caveat with all of that is that there are times when you need to call it and move on from a client that you've lost power with. This comes in the part of the relationship where you've either never had the power to begin with and you've always been treated as an employee or a freelancer, or you, for some reason, missed a lot of expectations or lost a lot of power and there's no way you're getting it back. My serious recommendation for when it comes to positioning is to delete those relationships and those client engagements from your life. Even if that's going to cause a financial strain, the impact that it has to your positioning when you allow yourself to be treated in a certain way with even a single client is going to impact everything you do with other clients as well. Consider cutting off any sort of relationship with any potential or current client that you have where you don't have a good power dynamic with that client.

Lastly, I want to talk about how to build confidence. Building confidence is part of positioning, because positioning is what your social media has on it. It is how you interact with the clients before you get them on the phone. It's how you talk to them on the phone and what kind of scripts you're using, everything like that, but underneath, all of those things come from a foundation of confidence. The best way to build confidence is if you have results. When you can fall back on a tangible result, "I did this. This is something that I can hang my hat on," then you will have a level of confidence that can't be easily shaken by maybe results that didn't go as well, or people saying certain things about you, or talking to you, or talking about you behind your back. All the things that kind of degrade your confidence, you can always fall back on solid results.

Now, if you do not have solid results from your services already, if you're just starting out, or maybe you've had a really long run of not doing very well at something, then the easiest way to build that confidence back up on a bed of results, on a good foundation of results, is to get results for yourself in something. Try to sell an affiliate product as a copywriter. Try to open up a landing page as a copywriter. Use your own skill to get a result for something that you did that doesn't have any sort of client money attached to it, and use those results in getting other clients. By building your confidence using your own money and your own stuff, it's something unshakeable. It's something that nobody can point and go, "Yeah, but that client had something that this client didn't, so your results are invalid." When you do it for yourself from scratch, it builds a very, very strong piece of confidence. That's my recommendation for building confidence.

The Process Of Building Positioning

Because positioning is such a subconscious aspect of business and reputation, there isn't an easy way to "systematize" it. However, there are things you can put into place that reinforce and build on your positioning as an expert.

System #1 - Use A Scheduler App. The implementation here is simple, but the psychology is strong. When a person uses your app to schedule an appointment to speak with you, it does several things. It forces them to use your technology...thus, making them use your system and positioning you higher. It makes them commit to a specific time and date...which psychologically makes it more important to them. It also subconsciously makes them believe that you value your time enough to schedule it. And finally, it makes you seem less "available"...which is standard for any expert.

I personally use Schedule Once, but several of my students use Calendly. Use whichever one works for you. It's simple, cheap, and absolutely critical to re-capturing control over your schedule.

System #2 - Limit the clients you take. This usually happens by necessity, but it's important to seem "in demand" to maintain your positioning. I purposely only work with 2 clients per month, max. I adjust my prices and availability accordingly.

Ideal market

The number one question I use to identify what I would consider to be an ideal marketplace is;

If I didn't get paid until I got results, who would I work with?

Period. End of question. If I didn't get paid until I got results, who would I work with? The reason I use that question is, there are dozens if not hundreds of different services that you can offer as a freelance copywriter or as a client services business. All of those services have value to a business. All of those services can be done by people other than you, and some of them can be done better than you, but if there's something that you can do for a specific type of client and a specific type of project that you would be okay with working until your client got results, then that is going to be an ideal market and an ideal offer. Once you start asking that question, you can keep asking it over and over to get more and more detail.

When you're building a specific avatar and you're asking this question to yourself, then you can pick out the qualities of a client that you would want in order to achieve the best results. If you want to get paid

$20,000 for a webinar funnel, you probably want to work with a client who has an offer that's already converting in some other medium. You're not going to test a new product, right? Especially if you only got paid until you got results. It's a simple concept. It's a very powerful question, but every time you ask that question and you peel back the layers of what your ideal market is going to look like, you're building yourself a very specific avatar. Eventually, you're going to have a specific type of person in a specific type of business that is delivering their marketing in a very specific way, and they hang out on certain platforms or in certain areas, and you're able to accurately target them based on their actions and the different things that they do. When you're building that specific avatar, it's very critical to always keep it an organic structure, which means it's always changing.

If your avatar uses webinars right now, and that's the most effective thing for them, and they're trying to do that in the best way, in a year, or two years, or five years, that may not be the case, and so you can't remain romantic about your specific avatar. Instead, you have to constantly be updating and asking yourself, "If I didn't get paid until I got results, who would I work with?" Once you've done that, you can go about finding that avatar. Having a specific person you're looking for is going to make this step much, much easier.

When you find that avatar, it's because they spend time, they're a human who wakes up at a certain time during the day and goes to bed at a certain time during the day, and in between, they are doing stuff. That stuff includes being on their cell phone, reading certain papers or magazines, traveling, being in certain areas, listening to certain radio shows or podcasts. There are things that your ideal avatar does every single day, maybe once a week, maybe once a month, but the point being, there are things that they do where you can find them and you can reach them. You have to understand who they are before you discover where they are.

Now, once you've discovered who they are and where they are, you can go about understanding that avatar. If you've got a specific person, let's say it's a 35-year-old digital business owner or single mom who runs a blog, and she runs in a lot of Facebook group circles, she does a lot of Instagram and Pinterest, she spends time in her car a lot listening to the radio or podcast. She's with her kid. She watches a lot of Disney movies, and she cooks in her kitchen. She uses her iPad a lot. Now you know who that person is, and you kind of know where that person is, but do you truly understand her? Understanding your avatar is getting into her head and knowing what's a priority for her, what is not a priority for her, what turns her off, what makes her perk up and pay attention. What are things that will immediately discount you or discredit you in her eyes, and what are some things that will build you up in her eyes?

By understanding that avatar, you can move on to the next step, which is talking with that avatar. After you've understood who they are, where they are, and you get deep into the psyche of that person, then you can start to actually try to talk with that avatar. Now, when I say "talk with the avatar," I mean it literally and also figuratively. Literally, I mean if you can find a representative of your avatar, go talk to that person. Go see if any of the assumptions that you made are correct or incorrect, and start really fleshing out the idea of your ideal market from an actual conversation, an honest-to-God conversation. If you can't do that, then you need to start putting out advertising via Facebook Ads, via Facebook posts, via Twitter, Instagram, Pinterest, direct mail, radio ads, phone conversations.

Whatever you got to do, whatever medium you've chosen for your avatar, you need to talk with that avatar through advertising and see what they respond to. If they don't respond, they're obviously not interested in whatever it is you're talking about. You missed the mark somewhere, and you iterate, and you practice, and you go back and forth to talk with that person. Then once you've done that, you're going to start to realize that your avatar exists on various awareness levels. If they're aware of you, they're going to react differently than if they're aware of their problems versus if they're aware of solutions in the marketplace but not you specifically.

You need to map their awareness levels and figure out what they're doing, because if the 35-year-old mommy blogger is listening to podcasts, but she's listening to entertainment podcasts versus business podcasts, that's going to change their awareness level. That's going to change who they spend time around and what their priorities are. By mapping those awareness levels one through five using my Big 4 methodology, then you're going to figure out what are the best marketplaces to talk to your people, and all the while keeping in mind you're looking for ideal clients here. You're not looking for as many clients as humanly possible. You're looking for the perfect ones, the ones who can definitely invest in your services. Once you've done all of those things, you need to verify the assumptions that you're making about the marketplace. Especially if you haven't actually talked with your avatar and figured out where they're at specifically, then you need to go out, and you need to verify, you need to test advertising, you need to talk to human beings, and you need to make offers and see if people are going to actually go with them.

You need to establish a crystal clear person who you'd like to work with. Ideally, with a checklist of qualities and qualifications.

In the beginning, just list these out, and then measure each client against them. I recommend having an **actual** checklist. Here are some suggestions:

- Revenue from their business
- Open to advice and suggestion
- Timely in their responses
- Products I think are cool
- Previous experience with copywriters
- Previous experience with direct response marketing
- Existing traffic source (email list, ad budget)

Your ideal client shouldn't just be "whoever shows up". You need standards, and those standards should be written down. When you're starting out, those standards might not be as specific as they will be down the road, because you don't have the experience to know exactly what your favorite type of clients are.

From this chapter, you should have a clear **Ideal client Avatar** and a **Ideal Client Checklist** that you can measure all incoming prospects against.

Offers

There are different types of offers that you can make as a client services business. The first one is customized or bespoke offers, meaning that every single client that comes through your door, you are giving them a unique solution to their problem. The second one is a systematized offer. It means every single person who comes into your door gets the exact same offer. That's the McDonald's version. You go in, you order a number one, you get a number one. There's no changes to it unless you specifically ask for one of the slight changes that are allowed in the system. The third type of offer is the hybrid offer, where someone comes into your door looking for a specific type of outcome or a specific type of service, and you customize that specific service for their needs. For example, if you're an email copywriter, someone comes to you to write emails, but they're an eCommerce business and you typically work with coaches, you can make that hybrid account and make that work for them.

Now, here's why you need a few core offers. Your ideal clients, regardless of how specific you've gotten with them, are probably going to come in with various types of needs or at various levels of need, so you need a couple core offers. You need your big Cadillac package, the biggest package that you can offer to someone for the most amount of money. This is your 20, 30, 40, $50,000 package. It's everything that you could possibly need to accomplish whatever goal that you want for them as a copywriter. You need a middle of the range product, where you're basically offering one of the biggest conversion mechanisms to them and maybe some of the ancillary copy to make it work, but nothing as big as the Cadillac.

Then you need the bare-bones offers, the very limited types of services that you can do to kind of start a client relationship. These might be email campaigns, landing pages, or the script of a single webinar and nothing else around it. The reason I say you need a couple core offers is due to the fact that buyers like to have a choice, and when you have multiple offers that are already laid out in a system, it gives you a level of credibility and power and positioning that you wouldn't otherwise have. If you have multiple offers for a specific problem, it shows that you've put the time and effort into solving that problem for whoever shows up at your door, so you need a couple core offers.

Here's how to create a core offer. Once you understand your target market avatar, then you're going to start seeing that they have recurring problems. If the 35-year-old mommy blogger consistently has trouble building her list or has trouble converting people from her list into paid buyers, then you've automatically found out what a core offer needs to be. It's a conversion sequence for the mommy blogger. Every single niche, every single type of target market, is going to have a very simple solution that you can see as a copywriter to one of their core problems. That now becomes your core offer.

My recommendation is that you take that core offer and you turn it into your mid-range offer, because now you can offer the Cadillac version, which is an upsell from the core offer, and they get all sorts of awesome stuff in addition to what they really need, or you could offer the limited version and compare and contrast those and say, "Look, this is what I think you need, but on the limited version you'll get these results, which might be helpful to you." Now, a natural upsell to a core offer are things like ancillary services, are things like recurring services or optimization, or consulting on the backend, or all sorts of stuff.

One of the last things I want to talk about when it comes to offers is using good scope creep to increase the project fees. When a person comes to you and starts to talk to you about their problem, you're naturally going to want to offer a solution, but in this case, as a service provider, it's probably a good thing to continue to talk them through the problem and continuously say that you have more stuff that you can give them so that you can increase the scope of the project in the very beginning. You never want to just accept what the client shows up to you with. They say, "Okay, I need a landing page," and you're like, "Got it. A landing page is $500. Let's go for it." Instead, you want to say, "Why do you need a landing page? What are you trying to accomplish?" If that turns into a conversation around their new product that they're trying to launch, then you've now uncovered perhaps an entire product launch sequence that you can write for them rather than just a landing page. That's how you use good scope creep to increase the project fees.

First off, **eliminate anything you dislike writing**. If you hate writing webinars...don't write webinars. If you don't like sales letters...don't write sales letters. It's simple, but freelancers are bad at sticking to their guns.

Next, **create a perfect project**. This is everything you'd hand to your client if you had to make money from the project **before** they paid you...therefore, it should be your best work and total package.

You'll want to call this something cool. "Platinum Package" or "The 7-Figure Webinar Funnel Package". Whatever.

Now price it accordingly. If it'll take you 40 hours to write, and you want to work 40 hours a month and make $25,000 a month...the package is $25,000.

As long as the value of the package is 10x-100x the price you're charging, the price is irrelevant. Your ideal client should have the capital necessary to invest in the project...otherwise, they're not an ideal client, or you don't know your market well enough yet.

After you've created and priced the **perfect project** for your **ideal client**, you'll want to split that package up into 2 smaller packages. I like to use Core and Ancillary. Core = Just the webinar. The script, and usually the raw slide deck. Ancillary = The copy around the webinar that promotes the webinar and the sale afterward. Things like emails, ad copy, and registration pages.

These are your two smaller offers. Offer your Core offer at 2/3rd the price of the Perfect Package, and offer the Ancillary at 1/3rd the price. You'll want to emphasize that they work better together, but some clients already have a webinar or ancillary copy, and just want something smaller. No big deal.

Now you have 3 Offers: The Big One, the Core, and the Ancillary. You can also split things up differently if you want...whatever makes sense for your favorite kind of copy and offers.

For example, if you're a fan of email copy, your Perfect Project might be a 15 email long autoresponder sequence that sells a product. Your Core might be

7 sales emails at the end of the sequence. Your Ancillary might be daily emails. Think about your specific situation and adapt the principle to suit your needs.

Leads

Now, all leads are not created equal. There are bad leads, there are good leads, and there are great leads. A bad lead is someone who just wastes your time. They've raised their hand, they're interested in your service or whatever it is that you're offering, but they are not qualified. They are not good for your service, and they're literally just a waste of your time, and they will never be a good client, or they'll be a good client so far down the road that they're not worth spending your time on now. You don't want to invest multiple hours into a person who may or may not turn into a client five years down the road. Now, a good lead is a lead who's qualified. They're in your ideal marketplace, and they may or may not be ready to buy in this moment. Those are the types of people that you want in your circle. You want them following your social media.

You want them on your email list consuming content from you. You potentially want to talk to them on the phone and have conversations with them, because I'm not a fan of one-call closes. However, they're not people who are going to jump directly into your services right away. That is reserved for great leads. Great leads fit your ideal market avatar to a T. They're exactly who you want to work with. They have the money and the information that they need in order to make a purchase from you in order to enlist your services, and they're ready to do it right away. These are the great leads. You want to prioritize these leads, and you also want to create systems around prioritizing these leads, because instead of you trying to decide what type of lead they are, you can craft a system around them coming to you and identifying what type of lead that they are.

Now, think about this. Your time as a freelancer has a monetary value. Okay? That means that spending that time on a bad lead costs you money. If you're on the phone with a potential prospect and they are a bad lead, then it costs you hundreds of dollars an hour to waste on them. It costs you hundreds of dollars an hour to write emails to them and to talk to them on Facebook Messenger. Therefore, lead quality should be your primary concern, not lead quantity. When you're creating lead systems that bring in qualified leads to your business, the key there is quality and not quantity.

If you get 10 leads a month, and they are all great leads, that is a fantastic lead generation system. If you get 100 leads a month, and they're all bad leads, that is a terrible lead generation system. Presumably, you're in this freelancing thing because you want freedom, and sitting on sales calls all day or talking with clients all day and then writing copy at night to fulfill on any of the jobs you actually create, that doesn't sound like freedom. That doesn't sound like what you actually want from this business, so there's two methodologies that I would recommend to actually gathering and consistently getting leads.

The first method is the one that I use. It's a more natural, organic lead flow methodology. I do this through branding, and I'm going to talk about the how-to later on. The second best method is what I would call an aggregated source of qualified prospects that you can turn into leads at any time. My recommendation here is to do that via an email list, but you can also use resources like a Facebook group, a social following, or a public job listing platform if you want to work that way. The idea behind it is that an aggregated source of qualified prospects is a place where you can go in and tap into at any time in order to get the leads that you want. This, in my opinion, is a great way to go if you don't want to build the personal brand around your own services, and rather you would just kind of want to skate through.

First off, I need to be blunt: there are 1001 ways to generate leads. Most of those ways work. Some work better than others. But there is no "single best way", no matter how many coaches are screaming it in their webinars.

These are two options that I'd recommend to you.

Option 1 - The Branding Way

Right now, it's **free** to produce and distribute content on the big social platforms. With a cell phone, computer, and Facebook, I built my freelancing business into a 6 figure income in 2 years. No ads, no website, no lead gen funnel, nothing. Just content, branding, and sales.

The **Process** to do this is simple: it's called **Top Of Mind Awareness**. You need a specific content plan that will constantly keep you in front of your ideal audience, and that plan needs to be consistent enough to produce a steady flow of leads.

I recommend picking one social platform, and making it your home. Understand it's nuances and quirks, and how people use it. Then, start producing content at scale to attract attention and show your expertise. Tweak that content as you go based on people's feedback or lack of attention.

On Facebook, I built my reputation by posting answers to people's questions in a Paid Facebook Mastermind Group 40x a day for 1.5 years. It's a lot. It took me between 4-6 hours a day to do. But that was my marketing. And it's worked pretty well. You can emulate that if you want, or you can post answers to questions in free groups as well. Free groups tend to be lower sophistication, but your ideal clients are still very active in the groups they're a part of. If it's in your budget, I would recommend that you post in a paid mastermind or forum...just to add value to an audience of BUYERS.

Option 2 - The Lead Bucket Way

You're a copywriter, so you know how to create a lead capture page and a lead magnet.

Price

The first thing to understand about price is that it is elastic. There is no such thing as the right price for something. There is no such thing as how much I should charge for X, whether X is a landing page, or an email, or a webinar, or anything like that. The price is elastic. That's because price is purely whatever the two transactors agree to. Whoever is involved in that transaction is agreeing mutually on the price of whatever is being exchanged. One person wants the most money possible for their thing. The other person wants the best possible thing for the lowest price.

Here's the thing. People's values differ. Some care more about time than money. Others care more about quality or ease of use than money. Money is not the be-all end-all of value. It's one aspect, and it's not even the most important aspect in most cases, especially with ideal clients. With that said, lead quality has a lot to do with what you charge. You might be able to convince a person through good salesmanship to purchase something more expensive than they originally wanted, but you can't make money appear in their bank account to pay your fee, which means if they're not a qualified person, then no matter how bad they want to pay for your service, they can't make money appear out of nowhere, unless you want them to go in debt to pay for your service, in which case I would not call them an ideal prospect.

The first thing first. Get good leads, business owners who are running real businesses, who value direct response copy, and they will see a tangible ROI for any copy that you write. That is a good prospect. That's a good lead. Now, price your service according to your personal needs and what the market can bear. You have to take both into account. For example, do you want to make $20,000 a month? How hard do you want to work in order to get that $20,000? The hourly calculus of your project fee is important here. If you want to work 10 hours a week so that you can screw off for the rest of the day, then you're going to want to work, then you're going to be working 40 hours a month. If you want to make $20,000 a month, then you'll have to charge $500 an hour to make your monthly income.

Now, that doesn't mean you tell your client you're charging them $500 an hour. Instead, you price your projects based on the actual time it will take you to complete the project. If a webinar funnel is going to take you all 40 hours that month, then you would charge $20,000 for the funnel, and you would do one of those per month. If you're writing emails, then you'll probably want clients who are okay with you writing 10 emails a week for $5,000. The calculus here is simple. You take your desired monthly income, divide it by your desired monthly working hours to get your desired hourly rate. You take your DHR and multiple that number by how long do you think it'll take to complete the project.

As a caveat, I would personally build in about a third of the time for buffer time to how long you would think it would take on the project, so if you think it'll take seven hours, charge them for 10. If you think it'll take 10 hours, charge them for 13. This gives you breathing room in your process, but by understanding your desired hourly rate and then being honest with yourself about how long a project is going to take, then you can be very clear about the amount of money that you want to make every month and what you're going to charge people when they come for your services.

I'm a huge fan of standardized pricing, but with one major rule: **Never tell the client it's standard**.

I price certain packages at certain amounts. I do that because it makes it easier for me to confidently state the price, vs. "coming up with something on the spot". My standard rate for a webinar funnel is $25,000, and my standard rate for a VSL funnel is $18,000. I do that because it's a number that is acceptable and familiar to my ideal client, without being exorbitant or high enough to make my client second guess themselves. I know Dan Kennedy tells you that their hand should be shaking when they sign the check, but I'm not about that...having a standard, acceptable price just makes the entire process much easier.

Taking your 3 offers from before, figure out how much time it'll take you to accomplish the Perfect Project. Then add ⅓ of the time as a buffer. So, if it will take 40 hours, add 13 hours, for a total of 53 hours. Then take your Desired Hourly Rate and create your "Standard Pricing"

If you want to make $25,000 a month, and you want to work 40 hours a month, your DHR is $625. 53 x $625 is $33,215...so that's your standard price for a project that will take you 53 hours.

Based on your DHR, measure out how long it'll take to do the other core 3 offers, and then price those accordingly. Having standardized pricing takes SO MUCH STRESS out of freelancing. People have a problem asking for money...but with standardized pricing, you're just tell them what it is, with very little selling involved...

Selling

The most important thing to understand about selling is value over price. Value over price. When you're discussing a potential prospect, or, I'm sorry, a potential project with a potential prospect, the conversation that you have with that prospect during your messages, during your emails, during the sales conversation, or any follow-up calls, needs to be around value and not price. What type of value are you providing that business? What type of ROI do your services provide that business in exchange for the money? Because words on a piece of paper aren't necessarily as valuable as the one webpage, or webinar, or sales letter, or VSL that is going to blow up their business and potentially sell millions of units of their project, of their product. Value over price. Now, the best way to do this is to go through a selling methodology that I'm going to explain later on in this chapter using things like the 11 authority questions and the C3P4 framework.

The Selling Process

While you have a standardized price for your services, the **conversation** you have with clients is NOT about price.

The conversation you have needs to be centered around **value**. In order to have a value based conversation, you need to be talking about problems and solutions.

Here's the method I use:

1) Prospect reaches out.

2) I schedule a call with them (unless I want to qualify them, at which point I'll ask questions via messenger or email first)

3) On the call, I start digging into their business and marketing. I ask TONS of questions. I ask about goals and targets. I ask about existing results. **If, at any point, they stop giving me information...they aren't a good fit as a client**.

4) At the end of the call, I tell them that I believe I have a solution to all of those problems. I tell them my project fees are typically above 5 figures. If they're **ok with those fees, I proceed**. If not...I let them go.

5) If they agree to the fees, I'll whip up a contract that also serves as a proposal. I'll outline the specifics of my Perfect Project offer to them. I'll schedule a call to go over that project spec with them.

6)   On the project spec call, I talk about past clients, past results, and projected results from this project. I make sure I'm clear about the value of the project: ie, if they pay me $25,000, the project has a high probability of making multiple 6 figures or even 7 figures.

7)   I ask them if they want to get started. If they say Yes, I invoice them. If they say No, I dig to see if it's Price related or timing related. If it's Price, I ask why they said it was ok before. Sometimes, confronting them results in a sale. Other times, I've just outed a lying prospect and I save myself the trouble later. If it's a timing issue, I set up a schedule to follow up at a later date.

That's it.

I'm extremely detached from my sales process. I want 1-2 clients per month, **MAX!** I'm not trying to get 20 clients. I'm not trying to convert everyone. Just the best.

Tech

Technology in your copywriting business needs to help you and not hinder you. Especially if you're just doing this for yourself, then you need to use as little tech as possible in order to accomplish the main goal. My recommendations for technology are things like ClickFunnels, a email autoresponder. I use ActiveCampaign, personally, but there are plenty of others, and maybe some sort of survey software so that you can gather information. Most of the time, though, you're going to find out that just good old-fashioned Google, Google Sheets, Google Documents, Google Slides are going to be enough for you to get all of this stuff done. The more tech you add, the more complicated things are going to get, the more systems you're going to have to learn and master, and just in general, the more convoluted your business is going to get. For the most part, you don't need anything crazy or big in order to accomplish a lot of big things as a freelancer, even if you're going to sell the business to someone else.

I use Clickfunnels to create sales pages, registration pages, and email optin pages.

I use Active Campaign to manage my email lists and waiting lists.

I use Google Drive and it's software for everything else: lists of prospects, projects, research, content, etc

I use Schedule Once for my scheduler.

I believe that simplicity is the key in freelancing. Every single step adds 2x-5x the complexity to the business. Rather than a 10 step funnel, I want a 2 step.

At a bare minimum, I think you need the following:

- A scheduler app
- An email autoresponder (with corresponding link to join it)
- A social media profile, preferably on Facebook.

Business model

This is where we're going to talk about the two different types of businesses that you can create. Either you're going to build the business around being able to sell it to a copywriter, or being able to sell it to anybody. The first type of business model is just the copywriter model. This is where you're going to try to figure out the best way to automate and systematize your process as a writer in order to get the most amount of time, ROI, for what you do. Usually, for most copywriters, this means they're going to completely or almost completely automate the process of getting clients and closing people into work. That means they can spend the vast majority of their time actually doing the work and writing copy for those clients. That also means that they need to systematize the writing process enough that they can take on more clients, do more work, and get paid more.

This compounds on itself until you either decide you don't want to work anymore, or you've got enough money to invest in something that will take up your time and attention. That's usually how most copywriters go through their business. Some copywriters never stop writing copy, and they just let their systems go for them. For example, Dan Kennedy never has to prospect for a copywriting client, again, in his entire life, because he's created enough systems to where the clients are waiting for him to open up. Same thing with his delivery. He is very clear on exactly what he's able to deliver and how quickly he's able to do it because of the systems he's created around himself and the ways that he writes copy to do that.

The second type of business model is the agency model. This gets a little more complicated, because now we're taking you out of the picture as a copywriter. For a lot of people, especially copywriters who've mastered a skill, this is an egotistical hit. It means that it's difficult for you to let go of what you perceive as your secret sauce. It also requires you to really dig around and figure out what it is that you're doing that makes your copy so effective. If the answer is nothing, and you're just doing a normal copywriter's job, then that's actually a good sign for an agency. It means you can systematize everything around what you're doing in a way that makes sense and has probably been done before by other people.

If there's a specific way that you're doing things that's different from everybody else, then capturing the essence of that and being able to communicate that to a team of people in order to execute it is going to be incredibly important. This becomes a skill for managers and process people rather than copywriters. My recommendation, if you want to create an agency-style business as a copywriter who's mastered a skill, is to either take the time to learn management and learn how to structure a business so that it can live without you, or bring on a team member, or an employee, or an outsourced consultant that will help you do it. You should not try to do this on your own if your goal is to sell your company as an agency in the next couple years.

Niche

Now, I talk about niching down in your business quite a bit, whether it's for clients, or whether it's for copywriters. The reason I talk about it so heavily is, the world is complicated, and it's getting more complicated by the day. However, there are tried-and-true principles that you can apply to almost every single niche. The nuances inside that niche are what are going to make you a very valuable freelancer or service provider in that niche. Knowing that webinars don't convert as well for certain types of traffic in certain types of niches versus via sells is going to help you when you're in that niche, but you won't know that until you become a part of the niche.

My recommendation for you as a copywriter is to either stake your flag in a sub-niche of a major industry, such as, if we're going to go down, you can go into the health industry. You can go into the supplement niche, and you can choose workout supplements or fitness supplements like protein powder, and pre-workout, and creatine, things that help you work out better and more and grow muscle as your sub-niche that you are now going to work in as your primary focus. The reason I would do this in one of the big three niches, in one of the sub-niches, is, you can more accurately become an expert in that space, and you can do it faster if you've decided that that's the only thing you're going to focus on, because now instead of dealing with thousands of competitors and trying to get the feel for an entire marketplace, you're getting the feel for a slightly more narrow marketplace that's still massive. Billions and billions of dollars transact in those types of marketplaces.

I would not recommend going into a very, very niche market like underwater basket weaving for people who live in Zimbabwe, but the idea here is to find the nice balance between way too big of a niche and way too small of a niche. My recommendation is, if the market itself has above a 500 million to $1 billion market cap inside its industry around the globe, then that's probably a really good size. If they're getting into the 50 to 100 billion, or if they're getting into the 100 million or $50 million range, the market's probably not big enough to support a copywriter who's specifically niched to it unless you truly commit to the size of that niche and you become the only person who writes copy for luxury yacht dealers, and that's how you create your career. It could be possible, if you want to do that, but my recommendation is to go right in the middle.

Proposals

A proposal should be a confirmation of the conversation you've already had regarding project scope and price. They should not be a decision point. It should be a foregone conclusion that the person is going to receive the proposal and say "yes." Here's how you do that. Number one, during your sales conversation, and after you've had the conversation that they are saying "yes" to working with you and you're going over the specifics of the deliverables, then you send an email confirming what you talked about on that call, and then if you have to have a proposal in writing for most, accounting or for invoicing or whatever, you go over that proposal on the phone and confirm with them and get payment before you send anything to get signed.

Contracts

This is a boring but incredibly important part of systematizing your copywriting business. If you do not have a standard contract that you use for every client that can be easily modified and sent out that protects you and saves you from bad clients or bad stuff happening, then you are doing your business a massive, massive disservice and potentially costing yourself thousands and thousands of dollars. Getting a contract written specific to your business, either through the services of an attorney or customizing one of the many templates that's available on the internet, you must, must have this. It is a requirement. I would insist that you use your own contract rather than the client's contract, because you don't have control over what the client puts in their contract, and you don't necessarily want to spend the time reading what their legal team has decided is valuable for you, because their legal team does not care about the conversation you've had around value. They care about being able to sue you into the ground if something bad happens. I highly recommend talking to your own business lawyer.

Expectation management

The most important part of delivering work is also the first part of delivering work, and that is managing expectations. The expectations of your client matter more, in my opinion, than even the deliverable that you give them at the end of the project. The reason being, if you don't properly manage the expectations of your client, no matter what you give them at the end, no matter how good it is, no matter what kind of result they're going to get from it, they're going to be unhappy. They're going to be displeased. Humans don't like when our expectations aren't met, and if you set an expectation and break it, you've lost all trust.

If you don't set an expectation and they make one up in their head and somehow you don't meet that criteria, then you lose trust. That's why managing and setting expectations in the very beginning of the client relationship is so critical to your success as a freelancer, as a copywriter, and systematizing your business as a whole. We're going to devote this entire chapter to exactly how you need to walk through the client's objectives, the project scope, how you're going to complete things, what milestones, what you're going to ask for. Everything that you can set an expectation for and meet, and how to create those so that they're not going to drive you crazy, and that they're going to give your client an excellent experience.

Communication

This chapter is all about communicating with the client. The way that I view communication with a client is proactive rather than reactive. Proactive communication is all about making sure that you answer the questions that your prospect or client is going to ask before they ask them. The reason I say "before" is, when a client asks a question, they have actually been thinking that question and wondering whether or not they need to contact you for hours, for days, for weeks, potentially for months, depending on the type of question. That is not a good headspace that you want your client to be in at all, so when you take a proactive communication stance, then you're going to not only make your client feel like they're extremely well taken care of, but you're going to halt a vast majority of the problems that most freelancers and business owners deal with when dealing with clients.

Clients just want to know that they're being taken care of, that their project is a priority and that it's getting done on time, on schedule, or before schedule, that their money isn't being wasted, and that they're not forgotten. It's really not that hard, and when you take it from the perspective of the client, you understand that communication and proactive communication is so important to their expectations and to making sure that they're happy with it that, again, it's almost more important than the end result or the deliverable. Every single human wants to be treated well, and just because they get a project at the end doesn't mean that they don't still want to be treated well.

Referrals

This is the chapter where we talk about how to engineer a process of getting referrals, and we're going to talk about concepts like top-of-mind awareness so that they are always referring you as the potential person for whatever type of copy or core offer that you're doing, and also a structured way of actually reaching out for referrals during and after the project is complete. The reason you want to actively ask for referrals and keep top-of-mind awareness is, most people will maybe have one or two people in mind if you ask them for a referral at the time, but they go through their lives, in their business lives, interacting with hundreds, if not thousands, of more people, so all of those people that your clients interact with are potential prospects and leads for you. Like attracts like. Business owners like to hang out with business owners, and so by orchestrating this top-of-mind awareness and getting actual referrals, you hit it from both sides and, in some cases, you never have to do marketing ever again if your referral system is strong.

The writing

Research, drafts, editing, and deadlines. This is where we're going to talk about how to systematize your entire writing process. We're going to break it down into three pieces, research, drafts, and editing, and then we're going to talk briefly about deadlines and how you set them for yourself and how you set them up for your clients to see, and why those two things are different. The research portion is going to follow the structure of my Big 4 research process and go down the line, giving you an extremely clear idea of who, what, where, when, and how you are going to talk to your client's prospect, and sell the product that your client is trying to make you sell.

The second part are the drafts and how to go through the draft writing process. I do say "draft," because most writers, especially copywriters, don't have a structured process of going through multiple iterations of a project. That's a bad thing, because if you only write one piece of copy, and you're constantly making edits to it, then not only are you being extremely inefficient with your mental productivity and writing, but you're also going to miss a big, big opportunity for consistency in your work. By making sure the systems line up where you're getting a quick first draft out as rapidly as possible and the best way possible, you're editing that for specific pieces and redrafting and redrafting, that is going to give you something to fall back on when you don't feel like writing or when you're trying to do your best work possible for a client.

The third part is editing. After the drafts have been created in such a way that you can really go back and refine, there's a process to take your work through and really get it edited down so that it shines and is polished to include the actual final deliverable for your client.

Testimonials

I always tell every single one of my students that testimonials are absolute gold. The reason why is because a copywriter typically does not get that many testimonials. There's lots of things in this industry that make a client want to sign a non-disclosure or make it so the copywriter can't talk about who they worked with or what projects they worked on, and due to the nature of the industry, a lot of people don't get the opportunity to get a good testimonial. So when you do get a good testimonial, you want to make it the best possible, and you want to put it everywhere. This chapter is all about getting testimonials, following up with potential clients who are going to give you testimonials, different ways to do them, and get agreements signed, and just in general trying to extract as much testimonial value from your client as you can.

Part 2 - The "How To"

Part 2 is where the rubber meets the road. Where the theory and principles become concrete, actionable steps that you can take every single day, week, month, and year to build a system that acts without you 95% of the time.

There are 4 Sections in the **Getting Clients** primary driver...and 6 Sections in the **Delivering Work** primary driver.

Each section contains certain steps that need to be followed, and when you've got experience on each, automated or systematized.

1. Section 1 - Content
2. Section 2 - Leads
3. Section 3 - Prospects
4. Section 4 - Sales

1. Section 1 - Onboarding
2. Section 2 - Pre-Writing
3. Section 3 - Writing
4. Section 4 - Post-Writing
5. Section 5 - Outboarding
6. Section 6 - Follow Up + Business Multipliers

Section 1 - Content

Step 1 - Create a content calendar

Step 2 - Produce content

Step 3 - Review content

Create A Content Calendar

The purpose of a content calendar is to remove the guesswork on what you'll be writing about and publishing. It keeps you accountable and able to track your progress towards your goals.The easiest method I've found is to define how many times you're going to publish (Daily, Weekly, Bi-Monthly, Monthly, Quarterly, etc) and then figure out how many pieces of content you'll need in a year.My recommendation is to publish daily if you're starting out. You have the time to devote to content if you're not working with clients. As you grow, you might slow your content production or hire outside resources to help you produce the content while you service clients.

If you choose to publish Daily during the week, you'll need 260 pieces of content. (5 days a week x 52 weeks in a year)

Break that into months, and you have 22 pieces of content per month.

My recommendation is to produce an entire years worth of Headline-style topic prompts, and then plug them into each day you'll write.

It'll look like this:

- Day 1: "How To Write The First 60 Seconds Of A Video Sales Letter To Capture 80% Of Your Visitors."
- Day 2: "7 Ways To Convert More Email Follow-up Sales"
- Etc.

I would heavily borrow from competitors, big publisher sites, and other resources...you don't need to reinvent the wheel, you just need to put your personal spin on the content AND publish consistently.

Produce Content

My recommendation here is to set aside a specific time every day to produce your content. Choose a medium: Audio, Video, or Written word, and commit to that every day. The goal is consistency, not perfection every day.

Review Content

Every month, review which posts got the most interaction: Likes, Comments, Shares. Make a note of that information and modify your content plan going forward to include more topics that are similar...people will respond to things that are relevant to them.

Section 2 - Leads

Step 1 - Create an email list
Step 2 - Produce daily or weekly content for that list
Step 3 - Review most opened/clicked

Create An Email List

I use Activecampaign, but you can use any email autoresponder. Some are even free up to a certain number of contacts. Then, drive the traffic from your public content to sign up for the email list.

Produce daily or weekly content for that list

Your email list is your "VIP" room. The content here needs to be *slightly* better than your public content, or at the bare minimum, more complete. If you publish daily, share about yourself and open up a little more. The idea is to create rapport with the list that is different from your public content.

n the same vein as your public content, you want to see what people are reacting to. Having a system to gather data helps you publish better information and course-correct f you're not getting the results you want.

Section 3 - Prospects

Step 1 - Create scheduler link for short, 20 minute pre-screening calls

Step 2 - Insert link into all emails from Section 2

Step 3 - Create 1-page cheat sheet for standard questions. Set scores for clients, and grade each prospect based on their score. **Good** clients move to next section. **Bad** clients get nicely put back into email sequence.

Step 4 - Verify prospect is capable of paying rates

Create scheduler link

use ScheduleOnce. The idea here is to have an easy way to schedule a discovery call with a potential prospect who reaches out, either via email or through your social media channels. It eliminates the time you waste going back and forth, trying to find a time that works for everyone.

Insert link into all emails from Section 2

This is self explanatory, but it also cuts down on the time you'd spend individually respond to requests. People on your email list can schedule a call if they want to, on their own time, without your involvement.

Create 1 page Cheat Sheet

My favorite list of qualifiers is:

1) Do they have the money to pay me?
2) Do they have a bleeding neck problem that I can solve?
3) Do they buy into ME and my value?
4) Do they have the ability to sign a check on the spot?
5) Does my service ACTUALLY help them?

If they meet that criteria, I move them on. If not, I tell them and put them back into the email list...they might be qualified in the future, so it's not good to burn a bridge by being dismissive.

Verify the prospect is able to pay your rates

During the sales call, I tell them my project fees are usually between $X,XXX and $XX,XXX, and then I specifically ask them if they can afford the project fees. If they say Yes, I move them on. If they say No, I put them back into the email list.

Section 4 - Sales

Step 1 - Create Detail of Project sheet (Proposal document) - use a standard Project and modify to client needs
- **Use a standard document for this. There are plenty of contracts to model online...pick on and modify it to fit your needs.**

Step 2 - Schedule Proposal Call
- **This is an hour long call to discuss your Project Detail over the phone.**

Step 3 - Go through Detail of Project sheet. Get a verbal "Yes" to move forward. "Nos" get put back into Email List or set up for follow-thru at a later date.
- **Have a payment link ready to accept the yes. Standardize the process.**

Step 4 - If **yes**, send standard contract and invoice together. Set follow-up schedule if contract and invoice aren't paid at 24/48/72 hour intervals. If longer than 72 hours, reschedule a call and discuss the delay.

Step 5 - Collect payment through PayPal, Wire Transfer, Credit Card, or mailed check. Verify payment before proceeding to next Section.

Delivering Work

Section 1 - Onboarding

Step 1 - Gather Resources from client:

- Testimonials
- Product information/access
- All previous copy
- Customer support tickets
- Imagery of product or product in use (or photos of the guru...basically all company owned imagery)
- Any/All market research previously conducted.

Step 2 - Conduct client interview. Focus on stories, ideas, myths, common misconceptions of the market, and pet-peeves of the product owner. Use a common Client Interview Script to get all information needed.

Step 3 - Set client expectations and give them a production calendar. Use a standard production calendar template from previous projects, that has built-in buffer time for the writer.

Step 4 - Give client a primary and emergency contact point. Primary = all normal business. Emergency = dire circumstances, like product production delays, launch delays, or project cancellations.

Section 2 - Pre-Writing

Step 1 - Research. Have a standard research document to track all research for each project. Use the Big 4 research methodology.

Step 2 - Compile resources. Organize by copy structure: headline, lead, body, offer.

Step 3 - Structure the copy. Headline ideas; Lead ideas; Body ideas; Offer ideas.

Step 4 - Brainstorming. Set aside clear time for ideation around the Big Idea, main objections and how to handle them, and stories to incorporate. Have a central drop point for all "misc" and brainstorm stuff that occurs during research phase.

Section 3 - Writing

Step 1 - 1st Draft. Have a set timer for the complete production of a first draft.
Total write through. Follow a template for this process

Step 2 - 2nd Draft. Clean the first draft using a rubric and template.
Add/subtract/adjust ideas. If it's unusable, go back to Step 1 and try again.

Step 3 - Final draft. Clean for grammer, flow, and coherence.

Step 4 - Editing. Use Bond Halbert's checklist

Step 5 - Deliver to client

Section 4 - Post-Writing

Step 1 - Set an optimization schedule with the client, based on metrics from
launch or traffic.

Step 2 - Minimize edits based on opinion or 3rd parties by agreeing to a set,
small # of edits.

Section 5 - Outboarding

Step 1 - Schedule call with client to go over the final deliverables. Get verbal
confirmation from client on approval of all pieces. Send final invoice if needed.
Confirm receipt of final invoice, and then transfer final deliverables to their
ownership. If you want extra security, get them to sign a "final acceptance"
document indicating they are happy with the project and have asked all final
questions.

Section 6 - Follow Up and Business Multipliers

Step 1 - Schedule follow-ups at various intervals with past clients.

Step 2 - Schedule a "thank you" gift for clients.

Step 3 - Request testimonials and provide ideas, templates, or multiple options to get one.

Step 4 - Request referrals and contacts to others

Step 5 - Schedule proactive outreach for additional projects in the future NOW.

Step 6 - Get commitment and potential down-payment on a future project based on the client's needs.

Step 7 - Get written permissions to use complete or partial work in your portfolio and as samples for new clients.